HOME SERIES

HOME SERIES
FUSION INTERIORS

BETA-PLUS

CONTENTS

8   Introduction

12   A dream trip around the world
26   Transformation of a duplex apartment in Paris
38   Perfect elegance
54   On top of a hill
66   Le Paquebot: a modernist masterpiece by Marcel Leborgne
84   Chez Odette: a fusion interior at the countryside
92   Balinese inspiration
102   Space and light
110   Restauration of a tuscan *Casa Colonica*
118   A majestic palace in Marrakesh

P. 4-5
The sitting room of a harim in the Ksar Char-Bagh guest palace near Marrakesh. The palace was inspired by 14th-century Moorish architecture.

P. 6
One of the bathrooms in the same guest palace (see pages 4-5) near Marrakesh. Washbasins with fronts made from treated marble. Marble corner lamps (made by Bernard Henriot from Peau d'Ane).

INTRODUCTION

I n this new title in the Home Series we travel through the world in ten inspiring reports.

All projects have very different influences, but there is one Leitmotiv that unites them all. They combine colours, textures, interior styles or cultural heritage in a contemporary setting.

An amazing and adventurous trip from Morocco to Tuscany, from the Mediterranean to Paris, staying in Antwerp, Brussels, ...

P. 8
Ksar Char-Bagh's tower staircase. The lantern was made by a smith in the Medina.

P. 10-11
Cy Peys has created a warm atmosphere, mixing styles and cultures in this Antwerp villa.
Dark tinted oak floors and wenge furniture.

A DREAM TRIP AROUND THE WORLD

Designer Lionel Jadot has created a very special interior for a couple with teenage children in a 6-hectare park on the outskirts of Brussels.

Transformed by the architects A.R.P.E. (Antoine de Radiguès) and the general construction firm Macors, this New England-style manor house is dedicated to harmony.

Objects sourced from each corner of the world can be seen in every living space: this is a real fusion interior, a dream trip around the world.

The interior decoration has been entrusted entirely to Lionel Jadot. Part of the living room is taken up by a table with a leather patchwork (from Vanhamme). A set of different coloured cushions adds a touch of brightness to the large sofa (also from Vanhamme). The open fire is ready for use when the temperature cools down in the evenings. The floor has been recovered from an 18th century building (work carried out by Thienpondt).

The office of the lady of the house is also home to an infinite number of hunting objects – one of the owner's passions.

The comfortable TV lounge.

The office of the master of the house is bright, open and has a warm feel to it.

The corridor leading to the office of the master of the house is entirely paved with bricks set on their side, as in the entrance hall.

In the basement, the swimming pool is located next to the steam room. The ceiling is arched and the ambience exudes tranquillity. The walls are made from tadelakt and the marble mosaic tiles take their inspiration from the tiles in the Saint-Marc Basilica.

The master bedroom with a bed from Vanhamme. Chinese lanterns provide the lighting.
A large doorway in the bedroom opens onto the garden and the terrace jacuzzi.

The teenager daughter's bedroom. The explosion of bright colours is dominated by rose and orange. To please the young lady who sleeps in this room, Mondrian's work, slightly revised and updated, is on view.

The boy's bedroom is situated opposite his sister's room.

TRANSFORMATION

OF A DUPLEX APARTMENT IN PARIS

I nterior architect Sarah Lavoine was given a carte blanche for this project in the heart of Paris: the transformation of a duplex apartment with 250 m² and 200 m² of terraces.

The renovation works took a long time because the original kitchen and entrance hall were situated on the upper floor.

Sarah Lavoine designed these rooms below, so the eighth floor could be devoted completely to the master bedroom with desk, dressing room, bathroom and wet room.

A Zen feeling of space and transparency in the entrance hall. The oak parquet floor was painted white and contrasts with the black elements.
A carpet on the stairs by Hartley, Pouenat wall lamp and "La Chaise" armchair by Eames.

A contemporary living environment in a loft style, with hi-tech and home automation. The coffee table was found at an antiques dealer. In the background above, the terrace with the black wall panels and bright red terracotta pot by Domani.

The Boffi kitchen is conceived as a library, with sliding doors in khaki-coloured paint.
Taborets by Sempre at the bar in black-coloured oak.

P.30
The benches and the dinner table were designed by Sarah Lavoine. A beautiful chandelier by Kevin Reilly.

The master bedroom is central in the open area on the upper floor to increase the feeling of space and make circulation around it possible.

The desk behind it also serves as a headboard.

Dressing room in a combination of grey and black-coloured oak with a low cupboard made to measure for storing shirts. A very comfortable fitted carpet in natural linen. The large mirror reflects the terraces. Hanging lamps by Sarah Lavoine. The bed linen and the cover are from Sarah Lavoine's decoration company "Chez Zoé".

A sober, monochrome space in taupe-coloured Azul Valverde stone for this main bathroom. The wasbasins are carved in natural stone. In the background is a large glass wall with mirror effect that hides the wet room.

PERFECT ELEGANCE

This 230 m² apartment in the heart of the 17th arrondissement in Paris, close to the Parc Monceau, is part of a beautiful property dating from 1910 with backyard.

Interior designer Romeo Sozzi, the founder and owner of Promemoria, designs 10 to 15 new pieces every year. In his Paris apartment, Sozzi displays prototypes, limited editions and unique samples from his collection in a search for perfection.

The herringbone parquet floor in oak, beautifully tinted in anthracite grey, is in subtle harmony with the walls in light amethyst decorated with Haussmanian mouldings. One can see the passion for beauty and an eye for detail that have become the trademark of Romeo Sozzi. Valuable fabrics, lacquered furniture or specimens in rare woods, lamps with silk or parchment shades ... nothing but ultimate austerity and refinement, between function and emotion: this is the philosophy that Romeo Sozzi strives for and it is also the secret of the perfect elegance of the Promemoria collections.

The giant "Mondu" mirror in rosewood rests on a bronze base. Opposite, a bronze "Elisabeth" lamp on a "Venice" chest of drawers in wavy rosewood with bronze handles.

In the small studio are two "Augusto Alto" sofas that stand opposite each other, fully upholstered in grey velvet. The desk and the little bench are prototypes: elm, beechwood and parchment. The wainscotting has been custom-made.

In the small dining room with antique mantelpiece, there is a rosewood table with a bronze base. Above it, a picture by Vincent Penin. The custom-made bench is upholstered in parma grey silk. The "Isotta Basso" chairs, fully upholstered in velvet, have bronze handles that make them easier to move.

Every kitchen element that Romeo Sozzi designs is made as a luxury piece of furniture.

A large "Kyoto" kitchen cabinet with sliding glass doors. The fronts are finished in aubergine-coloured varnish with an amethyst-coloured varnish on the inside. Dinnerware from Gien.

P. 42-43
The dining room. An oval "Erasmo" table: top in rosewood and a bronze base. "Sofia" chairs in lacquered beechwood and upholstered in velvet. A "Cecile" reading lamp, a bronze creation with parchment shade and a "Bip Bip" side table with the structure and handle in bronze, a plateau covered in leather and a good-luck frog in Murano glass for Promemoria.

The studio. On the "Theo" rosewood desk with bronze foot and handles, a "Cecile" reading lamp with bronze structure and a parchment shade. A "Molly" chair in Mahogany-tinted beech, upholstered in a parma grey taffeta fabric. The drawing room is on the other side of the doors. A "Willy" footstool, old gold-cerused oak, a "Wanda" dormeuse, two bronze "Edo" tables on wheels. A "Balthazar" wall cabinet in Macassar ebony conceals a bar, the handle is a true gem, in hammered platina bronze. A "Topazia" armchair in lacquered beechwood and upholstered in glycine-coloured leather.

P. 48-49
The living room with "Augusto" divans,
a "Bassano Gueridon" with ebony and
bronze inlays.
Hassocks in "Coccolone" velvet and
IDA wengé standing lamps.
To the right of the window a "Pia"
leather and bronze lampshade, to the
left a fold-up "Battista" side table in
green leather and black lacquer.

P. 46
The master bedroom.
A "Frou Frou" bed with padded
headboard, bedding from Quagliotti. A
rosewood "Margot" bedside table, with
bronze base and handles. A
"Marguerite" reading lamp with dimmer
and a sandblasted glass shade. An
"Aziza" méridienne with a beechwood
base is upholstered in a violet silk
fabric from Sahco. A "Gacy" hassock,
covered with a flower pattern by
Rubelli.

47

In the friends room the walls are hidden behind "Giano" lacquered wall screens inlaid with leather. The velvet pillows are by Manuel Canovas, the printed pillows by Carolyne Quatermaine. A "Bilou Bilou" chair is fully upholstered in white leather.

An ebony washstand with a basin in silver-plated bronze. The bronze wall lamp with ivory-coloured silk shade next to the oval mirror adds a porcelain hue. Across from it a bronze "Gong" console.

In the main bathroom: a bath in black Marquina marble.

The floors and terraces on the ground floor are finished in flamed Belgian bluestone in a random pattern.

The work surface in the kitchen is in Azul Valverde. Plumbing fixtures in the kitchen and bathrooms are by Dornbracht.

The dark shades in the bedroom give intimacy and rest in this room. There is a large window opposite the bed with a view of the landscape.

LE PAQUEBOT:

A MODERNIST MASTERPIECE
BY MARCEL LEBORGNE

In 1929 the architect Marcel Leborgne designed the Villa Diricks for the then CEO of Forges de Clabecq: a master in the art of living who wanted to find the allure and atmosphere in his own home of the chic international hotels he often visited.

This "city palace" was greatly inspired by Le Corbusier at the front; at the rear this villa lives up to its nickname "Le Paquebot" (the passenger ship).

Almost eighty years after the creation the property developer Alexander Cambron and his team realised a remarkable rehabilitation of this unique example of modernist heritage.

The original architecture of the listed and reputed masterpiece naturally was respected completely but at the same time thoroughly redeveloped.

P.67-69
In the entrance hall the marble basin, the very tall mirror, the translucent roof (with built in artificial lighting) and above all the Escherian staircase complex draw all the attention: the allure of a grand hôtel.

Fabienne Dupont created a unique living environment in consultation with Alexander Cambron, equipped with all modern home comforts: home automation, ultramodern lighting, contemporary materials (Corian, LED, stainless steel, ipé wood, …).

A few design classics and artworks ensure an exclusive and timeless atmosphere.

Consistently integrating the modernist style and the materials of yesteryear makes this an exceptionally successful and livable restoration.

CHEZ ODETTE: A FUSION INTERIOR

AT THE COUNTRYSIDE

A s a homage to the owner of a small bistro in the village, the property developer named her new hotel "Chez Odette", a charming guesthouse with six rooms and a refined kitchen.

Two rooms, a suite and a conference room, a bar and a sitting room, all designed by Ensemble & Associés in close cooperation with the owner. Alisa Thiry was the creative director and 3ème Bureau the general contractor.

A place where one can rediscover the pleasure of the countryside, whether in front of the crackling open fire or nestling cosily in a rabbit skin bedspread …

The living room / library with a sofa and armchairs from Flexform in weathered leather. A coffee table in stained cedar and lighting from Pierre Frey.
A composition of old village views on the wall in the form of a hologram and realised by Matthew Andrews.

The hotel sitting room. Armchairs and coffee tables were found by the property developer. A Flexform sofa in weathered leather.

P.86
Library bookshelves designed by Ensemble & Associés and finished in stained oak.

A rabbit skin bedspread from Maison de Vacances. Cushions in embroidered old linen.

P.88
The suite in the annex.

BALINESE INSPIRATION

The interior decorator Fabienne Dupont was given carte blanche for the renovation of this indoor swimming pool: together with the interior architect Vincent Bruyninckx and her loyal staff she had full rein in this project.

The garden around was already planted with bamboo and this luxuriant, exotic décor was the inspiration for the swimming pool: a holiday feel in Balinese style, Zen and restful to give some sun during the long winter days.

Fabienne chose LED and neon lighting that was designed to create a warm whole.

There are fake and real doors around made from steel frames that sometimes serve as decoration, sometimes as actual doors to close off the shower, hamam, dressing room and rest area. These frames were filled with bamboo sticks in the same colour as the wall.

Everything is dark: black beams, large black paving stones in and around the swimming pool that give the water a beautiful dark green colour.
The pool was made larger by integrating stairs with a blower and a Jacuzzi. The stairs are used like a seat. The heating is concealed in a band with black stones. The dehumidifier is concealed behind the bamboo doors.
The ceiling in yellow crépi was covered with black, 4 m long bamboo sticks.
Letters were integrated in the floor and walls with gilded mosaics.

The bed in the rest area is upholstered in white leather. The art photograph is by Pascal Mourioux, lighting with coloured LEDs.

The hand basin is made from slate cut in the shape of a leaf, with a surface in coarse slate.

The hamam with starry ceiling and custom-made wash basin cut in bluestone.

The rain shower is covered with coarse
slate blocks, a wall with a waterfall, and
the dressing room is finished with black
corrugated sheets.

The TV-room with sofas and a pouffe from Liaigre, a carpet from Jules Flipo (Milleraies) and a work by Mouffe. Custom made bookcase in bleached and sandblasted oak with red painted elements. A Manhattan chair (Interni Edition).

The colours of the walls (Pierre de Lune from the Ebony-Colours range) are in perfect harmony with the parquet flooring in grey stained oak.
A custom-made bookcase in grey oak and chrome covered metal. Custom-made, hand-knotted wool and hemp rugs. The furniture by Interni Edition (Manhattan sofas) is available from Ebony Interiors. A lamp by Liaigre and light fittings at the top of the seating area.

The dining room is a large, open space with two sliding doors that make it possible to separate it from the kitchen. Walls painted with Pierre de Lune paints (Ebony-Colours), curtains in glazed linen, J.C. 1 wall lights in patinised metal designed by Gilles de Meulemeester. The furniture against the wall is finished in metal and buffalo skin. Table and chairs by Interni Edition and a custom-made, hand-knotted wool and hemp rug.

The poker room with a custom-made poker table. Meridiani chairs and a Milleraies rug by Jules Flipo. The artwork at the right (above the console table) is by Ela Tom.

The kitchen was signed by Gilles de Meulemeester and finished in red and greige painted shades. Red chairs by Arne Jacobsen and tabourets by Bataille & ibens. The artwork is by Florimond Dufoor.

The dressing room (also custom-made) is finished in bleached oak. Surfaces in piqué leather and a red tabouret from Promemoria. The hanging lamp was custom-made in linen. A velvet chair from Promemoria (model Bilou Bilou) in the background.

The master bedroom, with a custom-made bed in bleached oak and a padded leather footstool. Led-chromed wall lights, silk and wool bedspread, a carpet by Jules Flipo (Louisiane Confort) and an artwork by Florimond Dufoor.

RESTAURATION

OF A TUSCAN *CASA COLONICA*

In Italy, the principle of the casa colonica or tenant farm was well-known until the 1960s: the landlord provided the agricultural equipment, the buildings and the land to a farming family, with whom he shared the profits. The casa colonica in this report is part of an estate of more than 900 hectares on the plain where the Arno meets the Tiber: an area of former marshland that was tamed and cultivated three centuries ago by a few families, under the approving eye of the Medicis and under the supervision of their court architect. This explains why all the buildings on this plain have a strong sense of coherence and authenticity.

This 18th-century farmhouse was painstakingly restored by the French architect Jean-Philippe Gauvin. Isabelle de Borchgrave was responsible for all elements of the interior design.

A terrace has been created at the top of the outside staircase.

The new kitchen is intentionally very plain and informal. The 17th-century Venetian cupboard has retained its original patina. The walls of the sitting room have been painted in three different layers of colour. The furniture was mainly found at local antique markets.

The walls on the ground floor were painted white in order to brighten up the house.
In the center is an old Parisian street light. The curtains were hand-painted by Isabelle de Borchgrave on a thick cotton cloth.

Two side rooms in the former shed on the ground floor.

The new interior stairs were created by the current owners.

P.114
The "Turquerie" is the only room in the house that is treated in bright colours. Isabelle de Borchgrave's colour palette is clearly inspired by the frescos of the early Renaissance master Piero della Francesca.

Every bedroom with its bathroom has its own character, accentuated by the many happy finds that Isabelle de Borchgrave has made all over the world.

Worn materials, ancient painting techniques, floors that have been reclaimed from the original farmhouse: everything in this country house radiates an unpretentious, timeless charm.

A MAJESTIC PALACE

IN MARRAKESH

The Ksar Char-Bagh guest palace is hidden away in the heart of the palm groves of Marrakesh: an oasis of serenity, beauty and refinement at a distance of 6 km from the Medina and near to three magnificent golf courses. The palace was inspired by 14th-century Moorish architecture.

A few figures: 7000 m² of buildings constructed, 3500 m² for the private apartments, 4 hectares of gardens and three swimming pools. Twenty-six guests have a harim (small apartment) with a terrace or private garden.

The staircase, with its elliptical form inspired by 12th-century Italy, is integrated into this room like a painting.

The fumoir is devoted to the Havana, one of the passions of the man of the house. An enormous fireplace clad with carved plaster. A large cutting table from Indonesia and a Chesterfield sofa of an indefinable colour.
The floor is laid with large rectangular tiles of Ourika natural stone and a stone mosaic of small marble pieces and Ourika stone.
Walls in red tadelakt – the colour was inspired by an old leather book cover.

The library table and its reading lamps with bases made from red Agadir marble and upper parts in silver-plated metal. A treated door and white marble moucharabieh in front of a window that opens onto the office.

P.120
A marble bench and brown marble decoration. Niches with patinated metal lanterns.

A door that opens onto the Orientalist salon. A Bugatti-inspired sofa from L'Orientaliste. On either side of the sofa are old censers from an Egyptian mosque that have been made into lamps. A rare carpet from the mountains of southern Morocco.

Views of three *harims* or private apartments in Ksar Char-Bagh.

P.122
A sliding door to the large salon, with chairs made of dromedary bones and wood. An Astier de Vilatte table, a vase with an escutcheon in patinated metal and olive branches. In the background is an old Spanish chair.

The library, with more than a thousand books, is like a gallery. Railing inspired by the Medersa Ben Youssef in Marrakesh.

The staircase: *bejmat* floor (small bricks) with the central part in matte polished tadelakt.

The hammam looks like a Turkish bath with its many niches in red Agadir marble and tadelakt. The floor is warmed by a network of copper serpentines.

The relaxation space was designed like a tent. Shades of red and violet.

The entrance to the hammam with cedarwood doors and benches and a hanging lamp from Syria. Wall lighting by Bernard Henriot produced by jewellers in Essaouira.

HOME SERIES

Volume 25 : FUSION INTERIORS

The reports in this book are selected from the Beta-Plus collection of home-design books: www.betaplus.com
They have been compiled in a special series by Le Figaro in French language: Ma Déco

Copyright © 2010 Beta-Plus Publishing / Le Figaro
Originally published in French language

PUBLISHER
Beta-Plus Publishing
Termuninck 3
B – 7850 Enghien
Belgium
www.betaplus.com
info@betaplus.com

TEXT
Alexandra Druesne

PHOTOGRAPHY
Jo Pauwels

DESIGN
Polydem - Nathalie Binart

TRANSLATIONS
Txt-Ibis

ISBN: 978-90-8944-079-2

Printed in China